I0487616

THE FEDERAL RESERVE BOARD

THE WIZARDS OF OZ: THE MEN BEHIND THE CURTAIN

BY
JOHN SHANNON

authorHOUSE™

1663 LIBERTY DRIVE, SUITE 200
BLOOMINGTON, INDIANA 47403
(800) 839-8640
WWW.AUTHORHOUSE.COM

© 2005 John Shannon. All Rights Reserved.

No part of this book may be reproduced, stored in a retrieval system, or transmitted by any means without the written permission of the author.

First published by AuthorHouse 06/27/05

ISBN: 1-4208-6501-3 (e)
ISBN: 1-4208-6500-5 (sc)
ISBN: 1-4208-6499-8 (dj)

Library of Congress Control Number: 2005905367

Printed in the United States of America
Bloomington, Indiana

This book is printed on acid-free paper.

CONTENTS

INTRODUCTION

This book starts by describing the Economy in 1998-1999. It was a great time for American workers, American businesses, American investors, American government of all levels, and for the American People as a whole. "Surpluses as far as the eye can see" was heard from federal, state, and local governments at that time.

We then move on to the year 2003. The economy is in poor condition. We are in an economic recession. Jobs are scarce, companies are laying off workers, investors have lost a great deal of value in their stock holdings (401k's, IRA's, Mutual Funds, Investment Accounts, etc.), businesses are closing plants, cutting costs or going out of business. Even federal, state, and local governments are having problems. Now they are saying "Deficits as far as the eye can see."

I would like to show that the Federal Reserve Board more recently lead by Alan Greenspan as Chairman is the cause of this recession and very many more economic problems we have today. The depression of the 1930's, all our recessions, inflations, deflations, the massive job losses in this country to foreign countries, unemployment, underemployment, and a potential dollar collapse that is looming in the foreign exchange markets, are all caused by Federal Reserve Board policy.

We then describe the 90-year history of the Federal Reserve Board. In chapter IV, I point out and describe the many problems the Federal Reserve Board has caused over it's 90-year history since it was created and given powers by the Congress of The United States.

We then describe what makes up a wealthy country and what makes up a strong country and why it is so very important to be both a strong and wealthy country. We are a wealthy country, but we are loosing our strong country status.

We then investigate why the Federal Reserve Board makes so many mistakes. Is it by accident? Is it on purpose? What other agendas, other political purposes, and other reasons does the Federal Reserve have for their policy actions besides their stated goals of full employment, non-inflationary growth? Their record is not very good on these issues either.

Then we move on to solutions; what can be done to correct the mistakes the Fed has caused and what actions can we take to ensure these mistakes will not continue in the future. Make no mistake there are simple solutions to these economic problems. Will the Congress have the political will to make the necessary changes? In this chapter, we list the solutions to the current economic problems. Will the Federal Reserve Board listen? Congress created the Federal Reserve and gave it all it's powers. <u>It can also take some of its powers away</u>. Then we discus if the solutions are not heeded what the individual investor can do in "Chapter VIII Gold Investment, Insurance or both." This chapter discusses the importance of owning gold as both an investment and as Insurance. Would you not have life insurance, auto insurance, business insurance, disability insurance, malpractice insurance, homeowners insurance, etc.? Of course not!! In this day and age with budget deficits as far as the eye can see, trade deficits, balance of payments deficits, social security liability problems, and the massive amount of dollars held by foreigners (foreign banks, foreign investors, foreign businesses, etc.) hanging over the foreign exchange markets like the "Sword of Damacles", it would be foolish not to also have <u>wealth insurance</u>. It is important today more so than at any other time in history to have at least 5% of your portfolio in gold holdings. The mistake of not doing so could be catastrophic.

AUTHOR'S NOTE

The United State of America is a great nation. It is a great political and economic system. It has a great people, but history has shown that no nation or people stay great forever.

Nations and currency's give way to stronger nations with stronger currencies. The length of time a nation stays great is determined by it's peoples desire to improve and desire to stay strong and great. What we as Americans choose to do collectively will determine how long the United States will stay great, which I define as wealthy and strong.

This is the main reason I am writing this book. Many people write books (novels, stories both fiction and non-fiction, etc.) For many, the one reason is to sell a lot of books. Yes, I would like this book to sell a lot of copies, but the reason I am writing this book is to make a real difference, to improve this great nation. I sincerely believe the policies I advocate in this book are both needed and necessary to assure our status as a "great nation." I see a lot of economic trends that can only lead to, at the <u>least</u>, our loss of status as a great nation and, at the <u>most</u>, an economic catastrophe.

I love this country very much. I am an optimist, not a pessimist. It is not to late to turn the trends from negative to a positive direction. The massive job losses in the United States over the last 15 or so years, businesses moving overseas, potential dollar collapse building and other economic problems can be turned around. They must be turned around. There is no choice. I am optimistic and my motive is to make a difference to move this country in the right direction.

A recession, which is the Federal Reserve Board's answer to every economic conundrum (puzzle mystery, dilemma, problem), is unacceptable.

DEDICATION

To the American worker, American investor, American businessman, American government, and all Americans in the hope, writing this book will benefit ALL.

DISCLAIMER

The author disclaims any liability or loss incurred as a result of information or advice given in this book. This book is sold for information purposes only and individuals should consult their own investment advisors.

PROLOGUE

As this book is being finished it is April 2005. We have been in an economic recovery for approximately one and a half (1-1/2) years. Although I believe the recovery very fragile, the Federal Reserve Board is aggressively raising short-term interest rates.

The last seven meetings the nation has waited to see if the smoke will be black or white rising from the chimney of the Federal Reserve Board meeting room. I hope the Federal Reserve Board is not in the process of choking off growth and sending the US economy back into recession, because if this happens, the economic outlook can and will be a lot worse than most people realize. The Federal Reserve may not be able to pump its way out of the next recession, especially if it is this soon into this recovery.

THE FEDERAL RESERVE BOARD

THE WIZARDS OF OZ:
THE MEN BEHIND THE CURTAIN

BY:

JOHN SHANNON

CHAPTER I

1998 – 1999

It's the years 1998-1999. The economy is humming, jobs are everywhere, just about every company is hiring. You can apply to literally any business and you will probably get the job. Graduating from college in those years' means naming your price and place of employment. Moving up within a company provided great opportunities also. The American worker was doing quite well.

Investors were also having a good time of it. IRAs', 401ks' investment accounts were all reflecting the prosperity of the times. Trading stocks was profitable and providing much needed capital for new and expanding businesses. Investing in the stock market was providing investors growing wealth and retirement funds. The American investor was doing quite well.

Businesses were prospering. Sales were there. Where everywhere!! You didn't have to look under rocks, cut costs or lay off workers to make earnings grow. Everything seamed to be going well. Many businesses were considering expansion, building new plants or expanding existing plants. New businesses and new technologies were developing which provided jobs, profits, and greater wealth for the economy as a whole. The American Businesses were doing quite well.

Even federal, state, and local governments were heard saying, "budget surpluses as far as the eye could see." This was the watchword of the day. Tax revenues were coming in at record amounts because of the level of economic activity. Employees were having good jobs and paying taxes on their investments. Businesses were paying taxes on profits, both new businesses being formed and existing business. Investors paying taxes on money they are earning from any number of sources. Governments were not only finding their tax revenues going up, but their expenses were going down with more and more people on programs and assistance able to find good jobs. More tax revenues means more money to spend on the truly needy. The American governments were doing quite well.

So, why did the Federal Reserve Board raise interest rates quickly and drastically tighten the money supply, pulling money out of the banking system and putting the American economy into a sever recession? Inflation, inflation, inflation <u>may</u> be coming. Turn out the lights on the party, inflation <u>may</u> be coming. We have to create a recession and put people out of work because inflation <u>may</u> be coming. If you put a lot of people out of work, that will stop inflation. So says, the Federal Reserve Board.

I contend there were no prospects of inflation in 1998-1999. Massive productivity gains (increases of output per unit of input) were the norm at that time. That keeps inflation tame. Massive international trade (cheap goods from foreigners), that keeps inflation tame. Massive capital spending by business (the capacity to produce even more goods and services in the future) that keeps inflation tame. In short, there was no inflation threat in 1998-1999.

Another factor preventing inflation would be the Keynesian Calvary coming to the rescue. They would be cutting government spending to cool off any sign of mild inflation. The Keynesian Philosophy, as we know, is to increase government spending in recessions and decrease government spending during a boom. This would definitely have kept inflation tame. Even though we all know Keynesians' love to increase the size of government during recessions, but seem to forget the other side of the equation to decrease the size of government in a boom. But that option could have been used instead of putting the US and the World economy into a severe recession.

Then, why did the Federal Reserve Board put the American Economy and by the way, the world economy, into a sever recession? Let's ask the Wizards of Oz; the men behind the curtain to answer this conundrum (a riddle in which a fanciful question is answered by a pun.) Inflation, inflation, inflation <u>may</u> be coming is their answer.

Since the answer to the question has always been, and will always be, inflation <u>may</u> be coming, though others believe otherwise, we have to conclude that the Wizards of Oz may not know what they are talking about or there are other reasons why we, the American economy, and usually the World economy, are thrown into a severe recession at the whim of a very, very small group of people at the Federal Reserve Board. What other reasons could there be? Let's examine a few conundrums. The Chairman wakes up one morning in 1998 and puts out the rubbish. To his dismay the rubbish is not picked up. He is informed later that the rubbish man has just bought anew SUV. He has just landed a new job at the high tech company that just started up in the local area. He is trading stocks on line and is buying a second

4

home in the mountains. "Boy, he is doing just as good as I am" quotes the Chairman. Later in the day, the Chairman and a fellow Federal Reserve Board member decide to go skiing in the mountains. When they arrive at the ski resort they have to walk up the mountain trail because the low paid ski lift operator just got a new pick-up truck and has opened a small business in his hometown and is closing on a Florida condo he is purchasing. "He's doing just as good as I am" quotes Alan, again. "That's it, I'm putting this economy into a recession. I'll put back a line of people looking for that rubbish job and that ski lift operator job, you'll see."

We have all heard the argument that Americans won't take low paying jobs and that's why we need illegal aliens. This is simply not true. If no one took the jobs the wages would be bid up and they would not be low paying jobs anymore. And as mentioned earlier, productivity gains, cheap imports, capital spending (producing more goods and services), and Keynesians' decreasing government spending would keep a lid on prices while at the same time raising lower wage rates to higher levels. If that is not the reason to put the economy into a recession let us examine another.

A large pool of unemployed workers is good for the military. When there are no jobs people enlist in the military.

Well, that could not have been the reason. Who could have known we would be in a war two and a half (2-1/2) years later. Then what could be the reason the Federal Reserve Board put the economy into a recession without the treat of inflation.

The fact remains it's very hard to see why the Fed puts the American and World economies into a recession when inflation is not a threat.

In fact, the very act the Federal Reserve Board does in raising interest rates, tightening money, pulling money out of the banking system is in itself inflationary in the long run. I contend this policy of creating a recession when inflation is not present is itself an inflationary threat and I will explain why.

Let's assume a fixed population working at 100 units of capital (factories) in 1999. Every year the economy adds seven new units and three are obsolete for a yearly gain of four units of capital (factories.) Without the Fed's recession in 2003, four years later, we would have 112 units of capital in the economy. With Fed's recession in 2003, four years later, we have only 88 units of capital. Four years of no new investment because of falling sales during the recession and 12 units lost to obsolescence. In 2003 we have a smaller capital base, 88 units because of the recession instead of the 112 units we would have had without the recession. Given 2003 when the economy starts to pick up and hiring occurs the same population and money supply matches with 88 units of capital is clearly very potentially inflationary as compared to 112 units of capital (factories.) In short, a fixed money supply and population matched with a smaller capital stock is clearly inflationary. Thanks to Federal Reserve Board policy.

The Federal Reserve Board themselves are creating inflationary pressures, instability and unemployment. An important point to make here is if you have a Federal Reserve Board that is totally fixated on the Phillips curve. They will create a recession every time we get near a capital investment cycle, thinking we are going to have inflation. Instead they should look at capital investment as adding more capacity to produce goods and services thereby reducing inflation, rather than looking at capital investment as adding more spending to a fixed capital base.

Here is a simple example of what I mean. Let's suppose on Gilligan's Island there are $1,000 total money supply and 2 huts and 2 canoes total goods in the economy. Goods and services equal money supply, so the value of the 2 huts and 2 canoes equals $1,000. Person "A" has all $1,000, which he deposits in the Island Bank. Person "B" wants to borrow the $1,000 to buy a hut and canoe (consumer loan.) Person "C" wants to borrow the $1,000 to build a canoe factory (Investment Loan.) If the bank lends the $1,000 to "B" (consumer loan) the bank has created money, an additional $1,000 as stated in any economic textbook. Now there is $2,000 in the economy chasing the same goods. Prices could <u>double</u>. But instead if the bank loans the $1,000 to Person "C" (investment Loan) the bank has still created an additional $1,000. But now we have $2,000 chasing one canoe factory worth $1,000 and two huts and two canoes worth $1,000, prices have <u>not</u> risen. In fact the canoe factory now producing canoes (faster than our canoe hand builder) will add more goods to our island economy generating real wealth for the islanders.

More goods added to the economy with the $2,000 money supply, prices could actually fall. The islanders will be much better off if the bank lends to Person "C" (investment loan) instead of causing a recession in anticipation of the inflation that may occur if the loan of $1,000 to Person "B" (consumer loan) is granted. The choice is simple, more jobs more goods and services at a lower price, more profits, more tax revenues or a recession that has long term inflationary consequences.

Here is another example of what I mean. Let us assume the American economy is made up of one plant that is the most efficient and productive at 10 workers. 10 Workers in that plant are the most productive and will produce the most product at the lowest per unit product cost. 11 Workers at the plant will produce more product than 10, but at a higher unit cost. 12 Workers will produce even more goods and services but at a higher unit cost than 11. In other words, prices start going up, inflation. The higher unit costs are due to inefficiencies, etc. Weebles start bumping into each other.

We also assume the Federal Reserve Board has just put the economy into a recession because they feared inflation may be coming. At this time there are seven workers and three unemployed in the plant-producing product. The Federal Reserve Board now lowers interest rates and pumps money into the economy to get the economy moving upward again. The plant decides to hire one more worker. Now, with eight workers and two unemployed the plant is producing much more product and at a lower unit cost. The economy is getting better; the plant hires one more worker. Now with nine workers and one unemployed, the plant is producing much, much more goods and services and at a lower unit cost. Now the Federal Reserve Board meets and announces drastic interest rate increases to ward off inflation that <u>may</u> be coming. The Federal Reserve Board thinking if we add more and more workers to that plant, inflation will rear its ugly head.

The only answer to this conundrum is a recession, shouts the Federal Reserve Board. This policy and procedure has been repeated over and over and over by the Federal Reserve Board for far to many years and has brought on the consequences we are faced with today. I contend this fixation with Phillips Curve Theory that has permeated the Federal Reserve Board for many years useful, though questionable during the 60's and 70's, is outright wrong today.

Here is the reason why. Let us see what would have happened if the Federal Reserve Board had <u>not</u> thrown the economy into this recession. The Plant is humming producing product at a low unit cost. The plant hires one more worker. There are now 10 workers and zero unemployed. The plant is producing at its most efficient point. Costs are the lowest for the consumer and the business. Sales continue to grow and the economy is doing very well. The plant now has a choice of adding one more worker to the plant or build another plant. Adding one more worker will mean 11 workers will raise unit cost and be inefficient. So the plant decides to build another plant with 5 workers in each plant. Unit costs go down productivity goes up as each new worker is added to the plants. Soon there are two plants and 20 workers producing more and more goods and services at a lower and lower unit cost. By adding a second plant (capital investment), workers benefit with more job opportunities, business benefits with more profit, consumers benefit with more and more goods and services at a lower cost, investors benefit with higher stock values, governments benefit with more and more tax revenue, and foreign countries also benefit with a growing global economy.

The choice is obvious to me. Every time the American economy reaches the investment cycle in the economy, the "Wizards of Oz" should not be throwing the American and World economy into a recession. There are other options, it is not necessary and this practice is totally wrong.

I also contend that if this current trend continues businesses continually seeing this when facing added sales will opt for adding 11 or 12 workers (in our example) to a plant instead of building another plant for fear they will be vulnerable to the Federal Reserve creating a recession. If the Fed does not create a recession and lets supply and demand for money regulate interest rates, businesses would be more apt to add a second plant rather than keep adding workers to the same plant creating inefficiencies and higher unit costs.

The Phillips Curve is the trade off between inflation and unemployment.

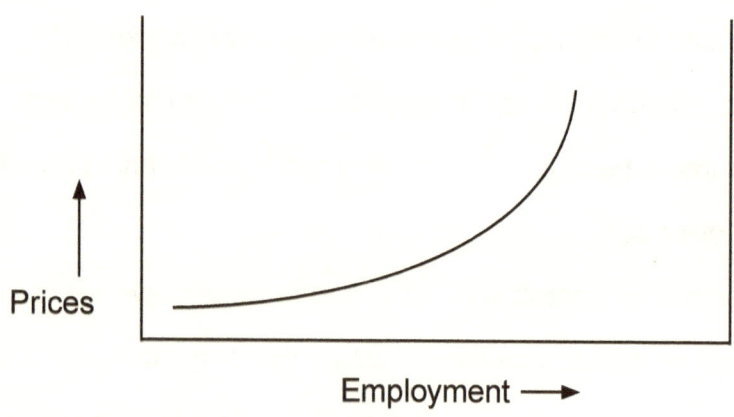

The Keynesian economists believe in a trade-off between inflation and unemployment. As you approach full employment, prices rise with a permanently fixed capital stock. This is true if you mistakenly presume a fixed capital stock. Since Keynesians are not very concerned about increasing the capital stock of the economy only the government spending, the Philips Curve appears to have some validity.

I thought the supply side economists of the 1980's exploded the Phillips Curve by saying if you add capacity (capital base) to the economy you could have rising employment without rising prices, in fact prices could actually fall. Apparently no one has told the Federal Reserve Board. They do seem to have a Keynesian fixation for the Phillips Curve. A recession, which is the Federal Reserve Board's answer to every economic problem, is unacceptable.

CHAPTER II

2003 – Thanks Alan

The year is 2003, the American economy and most of the world is in recession. Three years of worrying if you will be laid off from your job has made you cut back on spending. It is also very stressful to most American workers. Any and every business or organization and government agency could at any time announce cost cuts and layoffs. Companies are still lying off workers, will you be next? If you are, your chances of finding a job are not very good, not many other companies are hiring. Unemployment has affected many millions of people and their families. Unemployment is a real tragedy for the people involved.

But don't worry, you still have your IRA, 401k, and investment accounts. Maybe I'll go on line and check them out. Oh my God, what happened! My investments are worth 10 cents on the dollar. A fraction of what they were in 1999. In spite of that worrying, at least I am still working. Some others are not so lucky. Unemployment is up a few million people.

Companies are also feeling the recession. Many companies are no longer in business. Cost cutting, layoffs, slow sales, even years of losses are the norm. For the companies remaining in business, plant closings, buyouts, and mergers. This is terrible, Alan what have you done!

Federal, state, and local governments are also feeling the pinch. Slow economic activity translates into less tax revenue for all governments. "Budget deficits as far as the eye can see" is the mantra of all these government levels. To think just a few years ago we heard "surpluses as far as the eye could see." That was the slogan then, this is the slogan now.

Graduating from college in recession years means tough times. Careers are hard to find. Driving a cab or working at McDonald's until something comes up is not a great choice for most college graduates. The economy is not operating at it's full potential. Workers are unemployed. Plant and equipment is under utilized. The American economy is in a recession.

A recession. What is a recession? I do not mean the economic, government, Federal Reserve Board, definition, I mean the real definition. Real people millions and millions of real people loosing their jobs, loosing self esteem, loosing their property, loosing their wealth, loosing their dignity, loosing their dreams, and at times loosing their marriages. This is the real definition of recession.

Where could we have been? What could we have built? What could we have developed? What could we have solved? What would today be like with more capital investment in people, technology, medicine, science, etc., instead of recessions? I am just examining the United States. If we examine the World economy when the US enters a recession their problems are even worse. When the American economy is doing well, the rest of the world benefits. When the American economy is in recession, the rest of the world suffers greatly. Political instability often follows economic instability in other parts of the world. And political instability often means lives that are lost, at times many lives lost.

The way to reduce poverty in America and the rest of the world is to produce goods and services not to produce recessions.

In 2003 I could sense a panic at the Federal Reserve. The Fed had interest rates almost to 0%. Money was being pumped into the system at an incredible rate and the economy was still falling lower and lower, further and further, deeper and deeper in recession. Alan Greenspan and the Fed never admitted nor any financial journal or TV commentator saw the panic I sensed at the Fed during that year in 2003.

Was it the dreaded "liquidity trap" (money being pumped into the system but not used.) After all, why would business borrow if their sales were falling? Why would consumers borrow if they were afraid of being laid off? The Federal Reserve Board was in panic. Would this be the first time since the depression that they could not pump the economy out of recession? It could happen!! You could smell the panic in 2003 at the Fed.

Fortunately, the refinancing of mortgages gave consumers a lower mortgage payment and plenty of cash to spend. That was the financial savior that got the economy out of recession in late 2003. The Fed was relieved to say the least. The tax cuts did help to stimulate the economy, but the refinancing of mortgages was the major catalyst.

Hopefully the Federal Reserve will not raise interest rates and tighten up on the money supply too much and too soon, because the option to refinance which got the economy jumpstarted will not be available to homeowners until equity is again built up. The rising mortgage rates will also deter that refinancing.

With the economy picking up in 2003 there was much praise from congress and the financial community on what a great job Alan Greenspan and the Fed were doing to bring the economy out of recession. Hello, is anybody home? Did they not forget they were the ones that put us into the recession in the first place? The Queen of England even knighted Alan Greenspan during the recession. Either she is so far out of touch with reality or she is saying to Alan "great job Alan, putting the peons back in their place."

If the Queen of England can knight Alan Greenspan during the recession for his monetary policy then I would like to purpose that he be made honorary Emperor of China also in light of all he has done for the Chinese economy with his monetary policy. He can be the Emperor with or without new clothes.

A recession, which is the Federal Reserve Board's answer to every economic problem, is unacceptable.

CHAPTER III

Brief History of Federal Reserve Board

Let us try to piece together some of the reasons the Federal Reserve was created by Congress in 1913-1914. Let us say, in Guilford, Maine we have a mill called Guilford Mills. All the people in the town work at the mill. All the workers have their savings at the one bank in town, Guilford Savings Bank. This is a snapshot of most of America around that time period.

Suppose the Guilford Mills runs into financial trouble of one form or another. The mill is closed, a run on the bank occurs, and the Guilford Bank fails also. The town's people of Guilford are in trouble to say the least. No employment and no savings is not very promising predicament. The Guilford citizens suffer but no one else in the American economy is affected. The American banking system is sound the American economy is sound. Only Guilford is affected by this tragedy.

The problem occasionally when it occurred throughout America could easily have been solved with FDIC Insurance.

Having all banks at that time pay a small premium to the FDIC. Problem solved. If the Guilford Bank ran into that same problem and it had FDIC Insurance, everyone could be paid, mortgages would not be foreclosed on, savings accounts would be still there, the mill could reopen under a different business, etc. Instead, the Federal Reserve was created by congress and given far to many powers to regulate interest rates and create money. In little over 10 years the Federal Reserve created the largest and worst depression in history "The Great Depression." The whole American economy and banking system was unsound, unstable, and getting worse every year.

One very important point I would like to make is I am not saying the Federal Reserve Board should not have been created. It most certainly should have been created. The need for a central bank in the US and the rest of the world is all too obvious. What I am saying is it was given far to much power to regulate interest rated and the money supply. The Federal Reserve Board with its power to regulate interest rates is the problem. I am certain if the Federal Reserve had not been given the power to regulate interest rates, if supply and demand for money regulated interest rates, there would never have been the "Great Depression."

My contention throughout this book is that the Federal Reserve Board has promoted instability, unemployment, and inflation at the least severe recessions and a depression and a myriad of other problems at the most since their inception.

Let's go back in time 1913-1914. The Federal Reserve was created. It took about six years for the Fed to organize, setup shop, flex their muscle, figure out what power they had, etc., etc., etc. A very uneventful time Fed wise. But, during the 1920s' they started to lower interest rates (for that time period) and pump out money and credit creating the "Roaring 20s'." It was the Fed not prohibition that created the boom "Roaring 20s' and make no mistake it was a boom for that time period.

By 1929 the Fed had realized they had over stimulated the economy and decided to raise interest rates and tighten money and credit drastically (for that time period.) The economy plummeted into a recession but the Fed kept money tight and it turned into a depression. 25% Unemployment is a real depression make no mistake about it, all because of the Federal Reserve Board's mistakes. The depression lasted for years until the war in Europe, WWII, pulled the world out of the depression in 1939. History gives proof of the fact that in severe political instability or economic depression, extreme leaders come to power and wars occur. If that were the case, then the Fed's depression would surely be the cause of WWII, which I believe to be the case. Events influence other events.

Some myths need to be broke here. The war got the economy out of recession not President Roosevelt's spending programs. The Federal Reserve created the depression not the stock market crash. Extreme world leaders would not have come to power in good times. They often come to power in unstable times caused by the Federal Reserve mistakes.

Let's continue our journey with the Fed. The Federal Reserve Board did not do too much damage until the 60s' and 70s', some 30 years later. During this time period, the 60's and 70's, the Fed had a low interest rate, loose money, pumped out money like a drunken sailor policy partly to accommodate the war spending and partly to accommodate the spending of the new programs and big government of the sixties.

When inflation skyrocketed, the Fed would jam on the brakes like cars going by a yard sale sign. The Fed produced so many recessions during that period that one following the financial market knew what a yo-yo felt like. Due to the extremely loose money by the Fed of that period the dollar was considered very weak and very close to toilet paper status.

In 1979, because of the loose monetary policy of the Fed and the American fiscal policy, gold was soaring against the dollar and double-digit inflation could have easily turned to runaway inflation if something was not done correctly and immediately. The Reagan Administration under the advice of Professor Milton Freidman, a Nobel Prize winning economist from the Monetarist School advocated a strategy of steady money supply growth increasing yearly at a rate of growth of where you would want the economy to grow, say 4% per year, just enough to accommodate population growth and non-inflationary economic growth. This was a great policy and it worked. The inflation rate was coming down and the dollar was Goldilocks, not to week and not to strong exactly where it would have been for the whole Twentieth Century if supply and demand for money regulated interest rates instead of the Federal Reserve Board. It is amazing how free markets and competition work to put resource prices where they should be and not relying on one man's judgment.

In 1987 Alan Greenspan was appointed to the Federal Reserve Board. The Fed raised interest rates, the real estate market tumbled and people buying real estate in 1986-1988 saw their home prices tumble 30% in most areas. You could not sell your home until 1995, some eight years later at the price you paid in 1988

The Greenspan Fed kept money extremely tight (just the opposite of the 60's and 70's), so tight that the dollar soared to heights that are now unsustainable. And the strong dollar policy has made foreign goods very cheap compared to American goods. When foreign goods are cheaper we buy foreign goods not American goods. American layoffs occur and jobs go overseas. Yes, foreign goods are cheaper but if you don't have a job to pay for them, they are not so cheap.

The Federal Reserve with its monetary policy that has produced very, very strong (overly strong) dollar since 1990 is making foreign countries strong and the US week. This country will not be the strongest economy in the world for long with doggy walking services, massage parlors, finger nails R us, and McDonalds as our main industries. Sending all our industry jobs to foreign countries and expanding service jobs is a direct result of Fed policy. Whenever the economy gets near the investment cycle to expand productive capacity Federal Reserve policy is to put the economy in recession.

I know there are some that do not want rubber factories, chemical plants, and steel mills, etc, etc., and I can understand that. Let some other countries have them, but what was wrong with 1998-1999. High tech companies were expanding rapidly. Clean jobs, good high paying jobs, jobs that would keep this country strong for many years to come. That is where our strength is, high tech not fingernails R us. Those jobs were expanding in 1998-1999 benefiting everyone, employees, businesses, investors, and yes, even governments, until the Fed either exported them overseas or put them out of business. Thanks Alan, you are doing a great service to your country.

It is March of 2005. The economy is in an upswing. The Federal Reserve Board reports are all optimistic. Housing manufacturing, durable goods, personal income, employment, etc., are all improving from the recession. I hope these trends continue for some time. I do worry though that the Federal Reserve Board does not raise interest rates to quickly, which I believe they are doing now. I also worry that the Federal Reserve Board has done so much damage over the years with their interest rate policy that the economic problems are inevitable. March 2005 with long-term interest rates falling while the Fed is raising short-term rates, it seems I am not the only one who thinks the Fed is tightening monetary policy to quickly.

Now we are entering a great opportunity. It is 2005 and the American economy has been on an upswing for about a year and a half. Business is improving, sales are up, and hiring is increasing. The outlook is good for a slowly improving rebound in economic activity. And just as sure as the Federal Reserve should take the blame for causing recessions they should also be given credit for the upswings that they are causing. I do worry though, in their zeal to fight inflation that may <u>not</u> even be present, the Federal Reserve starts tightening money and raising interest rates to quickly and to much causing long term rates to fall (Alan's conundrum – a puzzle / a mystery) which is a signal by the markets that Alan is tightening to quickly and he may be putting the economy back in recession. And if that happens, home mortgage refinancing may not be able to keep the economy from entering a depression.

The answer to the conundrum may be that when the Fed is raising short-term rates to quickly, long term rates fall. When the Fed is raising short-term rates to slowly, long-term rates rise too much. And when the Fed is raising short-term rates just right, long-term rates will move in tandem. Conundrum solved.

In short, the next few years look optimistic for the US Economy and World Economy if the Fed does not choke off growth thinking that capital investment in the US causes inflation. Capital investment does not cause inflation it lowers inflation. The Federal Reserve causes inflation. The sooner that the Fed buries the Phillips Curve and stops fixating on it, the better off this country will be in wealth and strength. The loss of jobs, and high tech jobs in particular, in this country is a result of the tight money, strong dollar policy of the 1990-2001 Federal Reserve Board, which is the real inflation threat. A recession, which is the Federal Reserve Board's answer to every economic problem, is unacceptable.

CHAPTER IV

Damage Control / Problems the Fed Has Caused

Even though we should start with the problems the Fed has
caused, then move on to potential problems, I would like
to start with a potential problem that the Fed has created
because of its great danger potential. This danger I speak
of is the massive dollar crisis looming over the American
economy.

For 15 or so years, the Fed has pursued a much to strong
dollar policy. There is a "good" strong dollar and a "bad"
strong dollar. A "good" strong dollar is built on many years
of trade surpluses and balance of payments surpluses. A
house built on a cement foundation so to speak. A "bad"
strong dollar is what we have today, built on tight money
alone with trade deficits and balance of payments deficits, a
house built of sand and mud and a direct result of Fed policy.
This overly strong dollar, tight money policy pursued by the
Fed has results in foreign goods being very cheap in relation
to American goods.

As Americans buy more and more foreign goods, massive amounts of dollars are going to foreign countries in return for these goods. Japan, China, Taiwan, South Korea, and our other trading partners are holding these massive amounts of dollars that have been building up over the years. They do not buy our goods because our goods are too high with the current exchange rate. These four top holders of American dollars if they ever decide to sell dollars for reasons of portfolio diversification or they felt holding dollars was becoming a bad investment, the results would be disastrous.

When foreigners (foreign central banks, foreign investors, foreign business, etc., etc.) hold dollar assets, they do so because they get three gifts. Let's say they are holding US Bonds with the dollar rising as it has been over the last 15 years. Gift #1, they receive interest on the bonds. Gift #2, capital appreciation on the bonds with interest rates generally falling over the past 15 years bond prices have been rising. Gift #3 Favorable exchange rate because of the dollar rising. Foreigners receive in exchange more of their currency. Over the last 15 years it has been profitable for foreigners to hold dollar assets. But this cannot go on indefinitely. In fact, when the market turns the three gifts could turn into the three curses.

In February 2005, South Korea announced it would diversify its portfolio out of dollars, which sent shock waves through the financial markets. This could have triggered a financial panic. The foreign holders of bonds and notes getting a small fixed interest rate, Gift #1, would find that interest rate would not offset the massive loss of the bonds and notes values, Curse #2, due to the price falling. And the exchange rate of the dollar falling, Curse #3, would be a double shot to these assets values. Selling would start and the dollar could collapse in the foreign exchange market. Needless to say, someone must have spoken to the South Koreans because the next day they issued a statement saying they would not sell dollars only diversify any new holdings into non-dollar assets. If any large holder of dollars started selling, the dollar value would fall and other holders would find the asset value falling and they would sell also setting a downward spiral. This potential disaster is a direct result of past Federal Reserve Policy and the Fed must take the blame if this occurs.

Enough of the potential problems, lets get to the actual problems the Fed has actually created. As noted in an earlier chapter, the Federal Reserve has created every recession since its inception 90 or so years ago. That's all to clear.

They pump out too much money creating inflation, slam on the brakes creating recession. This is hardly promoting stability, employment, and non-inflationary growth. This was the Fed policy of the 60's and 70's.

The Fed policy of the 80's and 90's under Alan Greenspan is even, in my belief, more damaging although it is much slower unlike the quick stop and go monetary policy of the 60's and 70's.

Today's policy is far more damaging. Every recession we loose more and more good productive jobs and replace them with service industry jobs, like massage parlors, doggy walking services, weight loss scams on TV, etc., etc., etc. An example of this is a company I worked for in Augusta, Maine. For 15 years it was a Digital Equipment Corporation plant making PC boards for Digital Equipment and other companies. Although it was bought out by Sanmina - SCI Corporation, it continues to make high tech PC boards, fiber optics, and other products as a contract manufacture for other companies. The plant was beautiful; it employed 1000 people at its peak and nestled on over 100 acres. It was a great place to work. Good benefits and good pay are always a boost to the local economy. During the boom of 1999, the company was planning to add on to the building or build a second plant beside it. Then the Fed raised interest rates drastically. The economy dropped into a recession in 2001. Sales fell and the company announced a plant closing. Employees were devastated. Alan still has his job at the Fed but other people do not seem to matter.

The Plant was vacant for over 2 years. I heard the new owner of the building would be dividing and renting space to service industry businesses. Perhaps I can get a job there shining shoes some day. Maybe a dog groomer will open shop and there will be openings for doggy walking services. Services are necessary, but a nation of shopkeepers does not make a strong country.

An important point to make is building a second plant is not inflationary it would keep prices down. More goods and services per fixed population and money supply equals lower prices. Closing the plant is inflationary later in time. Less goods and services produced per fixed population and money supply equals higher prices. The inflationary impact of laid off workers on unemployment and other programs also cannot be ignored. In short the Federal Reserve Board is creating unemployment, inflation, instability, both economic and political.

Ask any general how important supply lines are. Many battles and wars have been lost because of supply line problems. A current battle may be going great but the victor is usually the general that gets the reinforcements and supplies to the front the fastest. Supply lines in peace time are just as important as in war time and possibly even more so. An economy based on services alone that imports all it's goods is like an army without a supply line. Depending on foreign countries for all its hard goods is economically vulnerable at the least and militarily foolish at the most. An economy is made up of goods and services. People may want services but people need goods. A nation may want services but a nation needs goods.

With General Motors announcing a loss for the quarter and other American auto manufacturers not doing well, where will this take us as Americans. Paper companies can't compete with foreign producers electronics companies moving to foreign countries. What is happening to our supply lines? A nation of shopkeepers is not a strong country.

Is the Federal Reserve Board Social Security's worst enemy? I believe so. In March of 2005, the Fed Chairman Alan Greenspan was before congress announcing that Social Security cuts are necessary. He stated the problems with the Social Security liability and informed congress cuts are necessary. When Alan speaks people listen. He has the power and influence to swing votes to cut Social Security payments and benefits. The fact remains that the Social Security problems were created by the Federal Reserve Board. Had the Fed not thrown the economy in recession in 2002-2003 congress would possibly be voting added benefits instead of cutting benefits. In 1999, I still can remember hearing "surpluses as far as the eye can see" by federal, state, and local governments at that time. I believe if the American people were more aware of economics and economic policy and knew the damage that the Federal Reserve Board has done to their investment savings, businesses, jobs (going overseas), IRAs, 401Ks, Social Security payments, etc., etc., etc. The Federal Reserve Board would be in hiding and shown on America's Most Wanted TV show.

Can real estate prices tumble? You bet they can. The year was 1986; the economy was doing very well. Stock prices were up, jobs were easy to find and the real estate market was profitable. Americans were buying real estate for investment purposes.

A couple of my friends were purchasing single-family homes, duplexes, six unit apartments, and condos, etc. for rental investment purposes. I told them to be careful. The Federal Reserve Board was raising interest rates sharply and we may soon be in a recession with real estate prices falling. Their answer was nonsense, real estate prices have not fallen in 50 years and all the experts were predicting real estate prices can go nowhere but up. And besides, why are you looking to buy a house. My answer was I have to live somewhere, I could be wrong and prices could continue upward. I also pointed out that I sensed a slight drop in real estate prices in the last recession of 1981. Real estate prices fell so slightly and for such a short time that no one noticed. I did. I sensed a slight drop in real estate prices during the 1981 recession.

I also felt the vigor with which the Fed was raising interest rates in 1986-1987 that real estate prices could fall much further this time. That is exactly what happened. The house I bought in February of 1988 fell in value by 30%. It was ten years later before the price rose to its original value. One of my friends filed for bankruptcy because of his real estate investments. Real estate prices can go down!!

So far in the recession 2002-2003 real estate prices have not fallen in fact they have been increasing. But the jury is still out on the Fed. The yeast is still active. If Alan stays true to form and raises interest rates to quickly as he seems to be doing up to March 2005, he could do a repeat performance of the 1988 economy and the real estate collapse he orchestrated when he was first appointed Chairman of the Federal Reserve Board in 1987. The real estate market and the economy did not truly recover from that recession for ten years in spite of the statistics pointing otherwise.

I have heard recently that the stock market bubble of 1999 caused the recession of 2003-2003. Just as I have heard the stock market crash of 1929 caused the depression of the 1930's. This is so utterly absurd. There was no bubble of 1999. The economy was doing very well and stock prices were reflecting that prosperity. If the Fed had not thrown the economy into recession and the economy was still prospering, 1999 stock prices would be a bargain today not a bubble. Stock prices equal the economy period. The economy goes up, stock prices go up. If the Fed drops the economy into recession stock prices fall. No bubble, just logic. 1929 was exactly the same. There was no stock market crash. The Federal Reserve Board's mistakes caused the economy to crash and the stock market followed. No crash, just logic.

Of course smart money does see the mistakes of the Fed and they sell stocks after the Fed raises interest rates and pulls money out of the banking system, but before the actual collapse of the economy. Due to the time lag giving the appearance that the stock market drop is causing the recession when in actuality the upcoming recession caused by the Fed is causing the stock market to drop.

The United States is at this point advising China to free their currency from being fixed to our currency. The US claims China does not have a free market floating currency if it is pegged to the US. The US claims it gives China an unfair advantage in world trade if supply and demand does not influence the Chinese currency. It is really very hypocritical for the US to say that China is regulating its foreign trade by fixing its currency. We are doing the very same thing. We are regulating foreign trade also because the US does not have free market interest rates. The Federal Reserve Board regulating interest rates instead of supply and demand regulating interest rates has the same effect of regulating foreign trade. The only difference is the Chinese want to export and produce goods with their policy and the

US wants cheap foreign goods with its policy. Not letting supply and demand regulate your currency or your interest rates has the same effect of manipulating your imports and exports.

The Federal Reserve Board themselves are interfering with and regulating US trade when they regulate interest rates. Our trade deficits would not have continued this long and pose such a danger to the world economy if the Fed was not regulating interest rates and keeping the dollar too strong.

Within a few years the trade deficits and balance of payments deficits would have lowered the dollar long ago to force US goods and services prices to be competitive. The purchases of more US goods and services would have eliminated the trade deficits. With the current Fed policy of regulating interest rates exchange rates are not free to self regulate trade deficits back to trade surpluses. Another important point on the Chinese issue, at least China's trade policy is helping China. The US trade policy is hurting the US. China is making itself strong, we are making ourselves weak. I can make a fair prediction if current trends continue. China will be by far the most powerful country in the world in the not too distant future.

Speaking of China reminds me of an episode many years ago. My father who never studied an economic textbook or took an economics class had a natural understanding for the great subject economics that I love so very much. Even though I studied and loved economics, at times he amazed me with his natural knowledge of economics and politics. It was the early 70's some time before Détente with Russia. The United States and Russia were the two super powers and were head to head on many issues. One of which was Vietnam among others. There was a lot of military tension between the US and Russia. I had mentioned to him that I wouldn't be surprised if we got into a military conflict with Russia the way trends are unfolding. His answer surprised me and I never forgot it to this day. He said, "don't worry about Russia. Their political and economic system will collapse from within. I will not see it but you will have to worry about China. When they wake up politically and economically, China will be the most powerful nation and the one most feared." At that time China was a country of peasants that could not even feed themselves. His thoughts on the matter did not provoke a disagreement only awareness that he may be right.

I made a call to my travel agent this week to see when my tickets for the cruise would be sent. It is April 2005 my 4th cruise and it is only three weeks until the ship sails. She informed me that she just got back from a trip to China. Her travel agency is starting trips to China and her and the owner of the agency wanted a first hand look at where they will be sending clients. She said, "John, I was in shock. The tour was nothing like I expected." She said, "I expected peasant farmers and dirty cities, instead I found clean, modern safe cities, beautiful new buildings, people dressed in suits going to work, in many ways better than in America." She said, "I was surprised." I said, "I'm not surprised." China's economic policies are designed to help China. The US economic policies with the Federal Reserve Board are hurting the United States. A recession, which is the Fed's answer to every economic conundrum, (puzzle) is unacceptable.

CHAPTER V

Strong & Wealthy Countries

What is a strong country? What is a wealthy Country? What is a strong and wealthy country? Let us examine some events in history. It is 1861, the beginning of the Civil War. The South had plenty of cannons, ammunitions, uniforms, wagons, rifles, supplies, etc., etc. So did the North. The first few years the South was winning the war. But as supplies were depleted all the production facilities and industry were in the North. The North could easily out produce the South in guns, cannons, machinery, ammo, and other necessary items to wage war. The South did not have a chance in the long run. The North was much stronger because of its greater industry. The South was a wealthy area prior to the war. It had an abundance of goods and services its citizens wanted. The South was not a strong area when compared to the North. Wealthy yes, strong no, when compared to an area it has a conflict with.

1941 was the year and the war in Europe, WWII, was taking place. Germany would probably have beaten the

British because of its superior industry and manufacturing. The Germans called England a nation of shopkeepers, which is the direction we as Americans are heading toward today. But when the US entered the war in the long run the Axis powers did not have a chance. The superior industrial capacity of the US could out produce the Germans ten to one in any category; airplanes, tanks, rifles, ships. You name the war material and the US could produce ten to one over the Axis powers. In the long run Germany did not have a chance. The United States of America was a strong country.

The American Indians were another example of a strong and wealthy people. Prior to the arrival of the white man they were a very wealthy people. Their culture valued a simple life of hunting, food gathering, etc. They had a great abundance of what their culture valued. Many believe they were much wealthier than we Americans are today.

The American Indians were also strong prior to the arrival of the white man. In relative terms there was no one stronger in their time and space. When the Europeans arrived that changed everything. The Europeans had the industry and technology of the time. The American Indians were still wealthy but not very strong in relation to the Europeans. The

American Indian culture and people didn't have a chance against the stronger Europeans.

When the Spaniard's first visited the Incas, the Incas basically had a service industry economy. Poetry, painting, dancing, music, jewelry making, who knows probably even doggy walking services were what the culture was all about. The Spaniards had the industry, manufacturing, and production of the day, so to speak. They had the armor swords, helmets, spears, etc., etc. and we do know what happened to the Incas. The Spaniards were a stronger nation.

I do not mean by these examples to imply that a country should be strong so it can attack other countries. What I mean is a country should be strong in case it is attacked. And this does appear to be the norm throughout history. History is littered with more conflict than peace and the stronger usually attacks or always wins if attacked. I ask for you to be the judge if you prefer to live in a strong country. I would prefer to be neither but given the only choice I would rather be a hammer than a nail.

What is a wealthy country? A wealthy country is a country that has a relative abundance of what its citizens want. The Incas were a wealthy people. So were the Spaniards. The Incas had what their people valued. They as a culture-valued poetry, music, art, dancing, etc. The Spaniards valued conquest, sailing, etc. They prized good swords, spears, helmets, armor, and the like. Both cultures were wealthy. The Spaniards were wealthy and strong in relation to the Incas. The Incas were wealthy and not strong in relation to the Spaniards.

So, a wealthy nation has a relative abundance of what its citizens want and prefer. A strong nation has a relative abundance of industry, production, manufacturing etc. that the nation <u>needs</u> in relation to other nations it may someday confront or be confronted. What is both strong and wealthy?

Since the word conundrum has many definitions, I would like to use one definition to emphasize the point of the chapter. Lets assume the US is the wealthiest and strongest nation in the world today. Wealthy because we have an abundance of what our citizens value, designer clothing, ATVs, drugs (both legal and illegal), workout equipment, movies, etc. Strong because we have an abundance of industry, manufacturing, technology, plants, and equipment needed in case of conflict that can be used to produce armament. A thousand space ships have just arrived on Earth and the American military is there, waiting for the space ship doors to open. The question is what will come out?

Since we as Americans are strong and wealthy in relation to all other nations in our time and space the opening of the space ship doors will determine if we will still be strong and wealthy. If the doors open and 100,000 aliens with bows, arrows, and spears come out we will still be a strong and wealthy nation. But, if the doors swing open to the space ships and 100,000 aliens come out with technology far superior to ours, the United States of American may find the same fate of the Incas, Aztec, etc., wealthy but not strong. Then we will be neither.

I guess strong and wealthy can be both objective and subjective concepts. The fact remains a wealthy country is wealthy if its citizens think it's wealthy. But a strong country is only strong in relation to another country in spite of what its citizens think. If the United States continues to loose its plants, and equipment, industry, technology and machinery to foreign nations, we as Americans will not be strong we will not even be wealthy. And our place as number one in the world will be passed on to another nation in the same manner as has happened throughout history.

A recession, which is the Federal Reserve Board's answer to every economic conundrum (puzzle), is unacceptable!

CHAPTER VI

Why Does the Fed Make so Many Mistakes?

Can one man be called upon to make decisions every day regarding where interest rates should be and be correct 100% of the time? I think not. If you think he can, possibly the Federal Reserve should regulate the price of corn, price of oil, price of doctor's salaries, and the price of new homes, etc., etc.

We have found throughout history that the market of supply and demand is the best regulator of prices. The price of money (interest rates) is no different. Supply and demand for money would have put interest rates at precisely the correct level over the past 90 years. Instead for 90 years since the Federal Reserve Board has been in existence, interest rates the (price of money) has been regulated by a small, very small group often influenced by only one member as is the case today with Alan Greenspan as Chairman.

I contend the past 90 years would have had a more stable level of economic activity. A stable growing economy with very few small recessions would have probably been the economic history of the United States in the 20th century. I believe surely we would not be facing the potential international dollar collapse we are facing today.

Of course we cannot tell for sure what would have happened but we do know what has happened. The Federal Reserve Board has made many, many mistakes causing severe recessions and a major depression. Events influence other events. World War II came out of the economic and political instability of the depression. We have had weak dollars, strong dollars, double-digit inflation, deflation, unemployment and underemployment. Not to mention the trillions of dollars of wealth people had that is wiped out when the Fed causes a recession, which makes the stock market fall drastically as in 2000-2003. Investment accounts can be literally wiped out.

The reason the Fed makes so many mistakes is because one man is making decisions that should be made by the market. The supply and demand for money should regulate interest rates not one man at the Federal Reserve Board. The Federal Reserve Board by regulating interest rates is disregarding market forces. Market forces of supply and demand for money are always pulling interest rates towards

equilibrium and toward a level of precisely where they should
be. At the same time, the Fed is pushing and pulling interest
rates where <u>they</u> feel they should be. Disregarding market
forces acting on interest rates is the cause of so many of our
economic problems.

The Federal Reserve has many duties ensuring a
slow steady growth of the money supply to accommodate
population growth and wanted non-inflationary economic
growth, clearing checks, printing currency, and many other
duties of which it does a tremendous job. But regulating
interest rates should not be one of their duties. The market of
supply and demand for money should regulate interest rates
not the Federal Reserve Board.

Another reason the Federal Reserve makes so many
mistakes is because throughout the 90-year history of
the Fed it, at times, has had other agendas, other political
purposes, other reasons for its monetary policy, which
at times is in conflict with its "supposedly" goal of full
employment, non inflationary growth. An example during
the 60's and 70's monetary growth of the money supply was
often linked to presidential elections, expanding to make
the administration in office look as if it was improving the
economy. Soon after the election, the money supply brakes

were put on and a recession would soon follow. Also, the Fed pumping out money at a rapid rate because of the Asian crisis of 1997 was more the cause of the 1998-1999 economic expansion than the newly formed internet spending (although that contributed also) contrary to popular belief. As we know the monetary brakes came on shortly after to produce the 2001-2003 recession.

Vietnam was a classic example of excessive money supply growth by the Fed to support the war. Prior to the Greenspan Fed monetary policy <u>accommodated</u> the administrations. During the Greenspan Fed monetary policy seems to be torpedoing the administrations with the one exception of President Clinton's second term.

This is indeed very interesting. There is no question the tight money, strong dollar policy of the last 15 years by the Federal Reserve Board is sending jobs to other countries. Is there a political purpose to this? Is it a way of helping the poor and developing nations? If it is, it is at the expense of the American workers and the American economy in the long run.

I assure you, I can point to numerous other examples of Fed policy linked to other agendas, political purposes or reasons for its monetary policy other than its goal of full employment, non-inflationary growth. Make no mistake

about it, the Fed can make or break the president, the Fed

can make or break the economy, and the Fed can make

or break your business, and the Fed can make or break

your country. The power to regulate interest rates must be

taken away from the Federal Reserve Board.   Supply and

demand for money should regulate interest rates. The Fed is

disregarding market forces when it regulates interest rates.

This page (107) reprinted below, is taken from a book,

"The Federal Reserve System – Purposes and Functions",

published by the Board of Governors of the Federal Reserve

System, Fifth Edition, December 1963. After you read this

page, you will find that it makes my point very clear.

Chapter VI

---

*INTEREST RATES.   Interest rates are the prices paid for
borrowed money. They are established in credit markets as
supplies of and demands for loanable funds seek balance.
Movements of interest rates are influenced by the nation's
saving and investment, by market expectations, and by the
flow of bank credit and money.*

---

*INTEREST rates are the prices paid for use of credit.   The
instrument of monetary policy have an influence on the economy*

in part through their impact on these prices. But in a market economy many factors go into the formulation of interest rates. They are established in the credit market by the interplay of the many forces of demand and supply, including the impact on credit supply associated with the use of monetary policy instruments. The pricing function of interest rates is to bring the supply of and demand for funds into balance. In this process interest rates influence the volume and composition of available loan funds and their allocation among competing economic activities.

After you've read the above page 107 reprint you will find that page is going to make my point very clear. First, I will divide the Federal Reserve Board history in three parts.

Part I: A grade of F- (minus) <u>hands on</u> monetary policy of 20 years from 1913 to 1933 causing the Great Depression and incredible Federal Reserve Board mistakes.

Part II: A grade of A+ (plus) <u>hands off</u> monetary policy of 30 years from 1933 to 1963. A magnificent record from the Federal Reserve Board as pointed out earlier no Federal Reserve Board mistakes other than what they caused earlier. No new major recessions, no new inflations, and no new deflations. Monetarily speaking a very stable and growing economy from the depths of the depression.

Part III: A grade of F- (minus). A massive <u>hands on</u> monetary policy of 40 years from 1964 – 2005. A horrible record for the Federal Reserve Board, inflations, recessions, unemployment as pointed out earlier.

The answer to the conundrum, why 1933 to 1963 was such a stable time monetarily speaking, is on this page (pg. 107.) After causing the disastrous depression, the Federal Reserve Board stepped back and let supply and demand for money regulate interest rates during this time period. Clearly reading this page, printed in 1963, sums up the Federal Reserve's stance allowing market forces to achieve equilibrium. I contend the Federal Reserve Board had a much, much, much, much more <u>hands off</u> policy towards interest rates during those years then today as shown in the wording from their own publication of that time. They let the economy function, period

From 1964 to the present they were all over interest rates like a hobo on a ham sandwich. Interfering with market forces and creating problems that would not have arisen if supply and demand for money regulated interest rates. Today the world waits each month for the white smoke to rise from the chimney of the Federal Reserve Board as they determine where interest rates will be.

I have rewritten the page 107 from 1963 to what that page should look like today in the current 2005 edition.

Chapter VI

INTEREST RATES. Interest rates are the prices paid for borrowed money. They are <u>NOT</u> established in credit markets. Supply and demands for loanable funds have <u>little</u> relevance to the interest rate level. The nations' savings and investment has no influence on the movement of interest rates and market expectations is ignored as well as the flow of bank credit and money. In short, Alan Greenspan regulates interest rates here <u>at the Federal Reserve Board and if you don't like it, lump it.</u>

I would like to present a couple of analogy's regarding the pre 1964 and post 1964 Federal Reserve Board. You and your family sit down one evening in pre 1964 to play Parker Brothers Monopoly. You open the game, pull out the Parker Brothers instructions, read them and proceed to have a good evening. Then, in post 1964, you and your family decide to sit down and play a game of Monopoly again one evening. You open the game and as you touch the instructions 7 members of the Parker Brothers Reserve Board appear. They proceed to tell you where to sit, what piece to use, which way to move what to buy, etc., etc. You immediately stop playing and decide to start planting your yearly vegetable garden. You remembered pre-1964 when you first started your garden. You proceeded to your local garden center, picked up your plants with a little instruction booklet explaining how to plant vegetables and you had a wonderful summer with a bountiful garden. But you know now it is post 1964 and you are not sure what to expect. You arrive at your local garden center but you are immediately met by a garden reserve board that must accompany you and help in your garden. The board picks out and purchases the plants with, of course, your money, accompanies you home and interferes with your garden in the name of helping you. You have a miserable summer with the reserve board but they soon move on and you start to pick your own vegetables. You find plenty of turnips, lima beans, rhubarb, and radishes, which you do not like and you realize there are no tomatoes, broccoli, and potatoes, which are your favorite. Whose garden is this anyway?

Another reason the Federal Reserve Board makes so many mistakes is because they have so much power to manipulate the economy. I have very, very, very, very, often heard people say "I am going to vote for this president because things have been good for the last four years" or

"I'm not going to vote for that president because things have been bad for the last four years." This is absurd. Generally speaking, the president has about as much control over the economy as I do. If the American economy is in a recession, Boom, Depression, Recovery, inflation, deflation, etc., etc., it is the Federal Reserve Board not the president who should be given the praise or the blame. The Fed is like the queen on an economic chessboard. The Fed can make or break the president when it comes to the economy.

In the twentieth century, I will admit though there have been three presidents that have made a material impact on the economy both during and after their administrations. Presidents Franklin D. Roosevelt, Lyndon B. Johnson, and Ronald Reagan. These three presidents did move the economy in a different direction from where it was heading. All other presidents in the twentieth century, their places in history, both good and bad, were victims of Federal Reserve Board policy. The president is the king but the Federal Reserve Board is the queen of the economic chessboard.

Given the fact that the Federal Reserve Board has so much power to manipulate the economy, because of its power to regulate interest rates, which is clearly the case we arrive at another reason the Fed makes so many mistakes.

Short run policy in economics usually has the exact opposite "long-term" effect. An example of what I mean is rent control. If the intent is to have low rents and we use rent control to keep rents low, in the long run, rents will skyrocket due to less building of rental property and obsolete rental property not being replaced. If the intent is to have a high rent area and we control the rent at a high price, rents will in the long run fall due to an over investment in rental property, excess capacity, etc. What this has to do with the Fed is the Federal Reserve has a lot of power to manipulate the economy. The Feds short-term policy goal sometimes has the exact opposite long-term effect or problem.

Some sixty years ago, congress passed high floor prices on wheat and other agricultural products. The idea was to keep prices high for farmers because they received such low prices during the Depression. At that same time congress also passed low ceiling prices for oil because oil companies made so much money during the war. These short run policies had the exact opposite long run effect.

Thirty years later, in the mid 70's, we as Americans had no oil, which skyrocketed in spite of its low price and wheat prices were collapsing in spite of its high prices the US had a surplus of wheat. Wheat was just about given away to

Russia and China or the choice would have been to dump it in the ocean. I contend that if sixty years ago congress did the opposite and put high floor prices on oil and low ceilings prices on wheat, the 1970s would have seen America buying wheat from China and exporting oil to the Arab countries. If supply and demand is not allowed to clear markets short run goals will have an opposite long term effect.

Suppose the Fed wants a low interest rate, easy money policy in the 1970s. That policy produced inflation and in the longer run interest rates skyrocketed. A short-term economic policy has the exact opposite long tem effect. My point is, if the Fed can manipulate the economy so easily and has short-term goals or policies it sometimes sets up the economy for long-term problems. Supply and demand for money would not have short-term goals or policy objectives and would not be governed by political purposes or other agendas. Interest rates regulated by supply and demand for money would be a far better choice than interest rates regulated by the Federal Reserve Board.

Could another reason the Fed makes so many mistakes be a narrow interest at the Federal Reserve Board. They are all bankers. We know that bankers are looking out for the banks, but are they looking out for the American worker for the American businessman, the American investor, or even other branches of the American government. In fact, I see Fed policy as having a very negative <u>long-term</u> effect on the American banking system itself because of its short-term policy goals. As I said, in economics short-term actions sometimes have the opposite long-term reactions if supply and demand is not allowed to function.

When a business has a long-term strategic plan it gathers together finance, accounting, marketing, production, and computer systems, etc., etc. Everyone gets on the same page and works together for the common long-term goal. What I see is a carriage being pulled by a team of 10 horses in the right direction. When I look at government and the Federal Reserve Board in particular I see just the opposite. I see a carriage and a team of 10 horses but the 10 horses are all pulling the carriage in different directions. Could this be another reason the Federal Reserve Board makes so many mistakes? A lot of its policies are at odds with and conflict with other government goals. Fed policy wiped out the budget surpluses of the late 1990s. The Fed policy often is at odds with and conflict with private sector goals also.

When I was a child we had pop up toys, a small table with holes in it. A hammer was used to hit one pop up and something would pop up somewhere else. You would proceed to hit that with the hammer and two more may pop up somewhere else. Every time I see one of those toys I think of the Federal Reserve Board. Putting out small brush fires. At one spot, in the process, igniting a fire somewhere else. Running to put that fire out ignites two more fires somewhere else. Their short-term forest fire management is creating a long-term forest fire catastrophe.

In mathematics one plus one equals two (1+1=2) always. In economics one plus one equals three (1+1=3) sometimes, one plus one equals two (1+1-2) other times and one plus one equals four (1+1=4) other times depending on other variables in the economy. This being said brings us to another reason the Fed makes so many mistakes with their monetary policy. Economics is <u>not</u> an exact science. If variables change the same policy can produce different effects at different times and at different stages of the business cycle. Supply and demand for money regulating interest rates will be the most effective and efficient way to assure rates will be precisely where they should be. A Federal Reserve Board cannot be counted on the make those decisions accurately and history has shown this to be the case.

If I am not correct in my assumption that the Federal Reserve Board makes mistakes by making wrong decisions by accident, the other assumption is the Fed makes wrong decisions on purpose. For the rest of this chapter I will take a facious and fictitious look at some very serious and real problems. Making wrong decisions on purpose more conundrums you might say. Let's assume this Fed chairman has a wife who is an international news correspondent traveling all over the world. She has seen many poor countries and less developed countries and always wanted to do something about it. Because "Americans have to much anyway." Over the many years as a reporter she has seen the inequality throughout the world, the haves and the have-nots. She knows the US government in the 60's and 70's just gave away money to foreign countries but that didn't seem to work. You know the adage, if you give away fish they will keep coming back for more fish, but if you teach them to fish they will fish on their own forever. So she asks her husband "what can we do?" Her husband, the Fed Chairman, tells here he can keep an extremely tight monetary policy, the dollar will get real strong over a period of years and people will buy lots of foreign goods. When people buy lots of foreign goods many, many, many, jobs will be created in those countries and lost in the USA. But that's OK because "Americans have to much anyway." The adage <u>says</u> if you give away fish, they will keep coming back for more fish, but if you teach them to fish they will fish on their own forever. The adage <u>does not say</u> if you give away fish they will keep coming back for more, fish, but if you give away the fisheries, the nets, the boats, the processing plants, manufacturing plants, equipment, high tech, etc., they will fish on their own forever. If you do that, then very soon we as Americans will be the ones begging for the fish.

Another conundrum. The year is 1980, a new president gets elected to office. The prior 15 years have been marked by many Fed mistakes; inflations, recessions, unemployment. In 1979 alone, the country is on the verge of runaway inflation if something is not done and done soon. The dollar is collapsing in international markets. The new president has a lot of new ideas spurred on by his economic advisors. They believe the Fed is the cause of most of the economic problems. By expanding the money supply at a greater amount than is needed for non-inflationary growth. The printing presses and money creating activities at the Fed has been on overdrive. The new president and his team convinces the Federal Reserve Board to tighten the money supply, raise interest rates, and strengthen the dollar which is much to weak. This policy turns out to be a great success. Many successes have been created during the period. At this time the dollar is goldilocks not to weak, not to strong, just where it should be. The economy is doing great in 1987. The president appoints a new Federal Reserve Board Chairman.

The new chairman knows of the success of the policy and he continues to stay the course. He charges ahead with tight money policy, high (real) interest rates, and a vow to fight inflation whether it is there or not. The president leaves office with things going well with the great economic knowledge that he and his advisors would soon have to discontinue the strong dollar policy after all the dollars have reached the correct level. Accomplish a mission is a reason to find another mission not ruin the mission.

But the new chairman is fixated like a dog trained to perform one task over and over, like a robot programmed to go in one direction. The robot cannot turn left if an obstacle is in its path. It cannot move back or left and right to avoid obstacles. It can only run into danger eventually. The new chairman acting like Don Quixote is on a mission to fight inflation even if the mission does not exist or is accomplished.

He charges ahead making the dollar far to strong in international markets. The strong dollar is producing job losses in the US. Jobs are being created in foreign countries, which means massive amounts of dollars are building up overseas. Building up and building up and building up. And just like our robot eventually running into obstacles, so will this policy run into economic obstacles.

Of course this strong dollar policy is inviting for the new administration elected during the 1990s. Foreign countries acting like hundreds of Santa's workshops around the world making sleds, stereos, boats, autos, toys, etc. for Americans. The world economy is acting like a giant Christmas season. The world is the North Pole and Americans are the children. In return for this Utopia dollars are being thrown everywhere around the globe.

Make no mistake about it, the dollar must drift lower, slowly and orderly as it has been doing for the past year and a half. This must continue. If the dollar falls to quickly or the Fed raises interest rates to much forcing the dollar to rise again the Federal Reserve Board must take the blame for the inevitable dollar crash that it is setting up in the word economy.

A recession, which is the Federal Reserve Board's answer to every economic conundrum, (puzzle) is unacceptable.

CHAPTER VII

Solutions / What Can Be Done!

The United States of American is a great country, a great nation, a great people, and a great system. It is built on the premise of freedom; political freedom, religious freedom, and economic freedom, to name a few. Freedom of the markets to guide resources in an efficient manner. Freedom in the markets means efficient allocation of resources, less shortages and less surpluses.

Central planned economies have been shown to produce inefficiencies , shortages, and surpluses. Goods and services not what the people want but what some bureaucrat thinks what the people want or what he wants them to want.

Do Americans have freedom of the markets in this country. I do not believe we do. Sure we can buy oranges rather than bananas or stereos rather than furniture and we can open a sub shop or a small business. But if interest rates are regulated by a small group at the Federal Reserve Board that is not freedom of the markets. Interest rates should be regulated by the supply and demand for money not by the gang at the Federal Reserve Board. I am going to say this loud and clear, the whole purpose, point, reason, function, desire, argument, plan of this book is the supply and demand for money should regulate interest rates not one person at the Federal Reserve Board. This is the whole problem. I cannot stress this enough, the supply and demand for money should regulate interest rates not one person at the Federal Reserve Board.

Lets assume its 1999 and person "A" just opened a small business. He saved money all his life to do this. Person "B" is just graduating from college and is looking for a career. Person "C" is retiring and has all her money in a mutual fund. Person "D" is married with three children working at a high tech company. The Fed decides to raise interest rates drastically because they think inflation or the boogeyman is coming. We are quickly in a recession.

In 2001 person "A" has just lost his small business and filed for bankruptcy. Person "B" with a college degree can't find a job. Companies are not hiring. Person "C" her mutual fund is worth 20% of its value that she was depending on for retirement. Person "D" was laid off and collecting unemployment at a quarter of what he was earning before. Is this freedom of the markets? I do not think so.

These people made economic decisions, economic risks, economic choices, and economic plans based on their beliefs of freedom of the markets. Would they have made these decisions if they knew the Federal Reserve Board would raise interest rates quickly and put the economy and their future in jeopardy. When I start a small business or invest for retirement in a mutual stock fund I find there is enough perils in the business world to contend with without worrying if at the drop of a hat the Federal Reserve is going to sharply raise interest rates and put the country in a recessions as it did in 1998-1999 to create the 2001-2003 recession.

Is this freedom of the markets? Are the millions and millions of people with billions and billions of dollars in assets lost because of one man's mistake. I do not think this is freedom of the markets. When the telephone company ad says to reach out and touch someone, the Fed should not take this ad to serious. Their touch is not always a welcome sign.

Let's assume the Federal Reserve had no control of interest rates in 1998-1999. The supply and demand for money controlled interest rates. Yes, interest rates regulated by supply and demand for money would have pushed rates higher, but not to the levels to create a three-year recession that the Fed pushed them to. They would have raised enough to keep inflation under control but not enough to create a worldwide recession. The supply and demand for money would always put interest rates at precisely the right levels as supply and demand does for all resources.

Relying on a small group to make those decisions is precisely why we are in the economic predicament we are in today. I must say this again, the supply and demand for money should regulate interest rates not one person at the Federal Reserve Board. This is the main solution to our economic problems. This is the most important solution to our economic problems.

I would like to try to imagine what it would look like in March of 2005 if in 1998-1999 the Federal Reserve Board has not raised interest rates and put the economy into a recession. Supply and demand for money regulated interest rates in 1999 so here we are in March 2005 with the economy still expanding. This has been going on since the early 90s. The stock market has not crashed so people have a lot of savings in their investment accounts. Their portfolios look pretty good. Most companies are hiring and good paying jobs are available. Businesses are doing well, investors, employees and governments also. There is no talk of social security problems because "budget surpluses as far as the eye can see" has been in effect since 1998 or so. The economy is not overheating because the Fed is not having interest rates to low and pumping out too much money. The economy is not moving downward because the Fed is not having rates to high and pulling money and credit out of the banking system. The economy is Goldilocks, just right.

"Money supply matters" and "Free market interest rates matter." The monetarists and supply side economists advising the Regan Administration in the early 1980s had the financial problems of the American economy half solved. These economists advocated a slow steady growth in the money supply. This was a good policy and only half solved the problems we are facing today in the year 2005. I contend that if those economists had matched that policy with a policy of supply and demand for money regulating interest rates instead of the Federal Reserve Board regulating interest rates. The economy today 25 years later would be stronger and not laced with all the crisis's we are faced with today.

Interest rates free to move by market forces during those 25 years would have eliminated the trade deficits, balance of payments deficit, and solved the Social Security liability and budget deficits with a growing economy not punctured by recessions created by the Federal Reserve Board trying to play pin the interest rate tail on the donkey.

Any overheating of the economy that may occur, though unlikely with money supply matters and free market interest rates matters, could be cooled in two ways; one, the Keynesian Economists would advocate cutting government spending to cool an overheating economy; two, the Federal Reserve Board could jawbone banks to step up loans for capital investment and reduce consumption loans. These two policies would cool down any (if any) overheated economy and are surely a much better alternative than throwing the American Economy and World economy into a severe recession. To make all Americans wealthy we must produce goods and services not recessions.

In fact, I believe most certainly that the Federal Reserve Board in 1998-1999 should not have thrown the economy into recession. Instead, should have jawboned banks to drastically slow down consumer loans and increases any investment loans. I see as a no-brainer, consumption loans being stepped up during a recession to stimulate consumption to accelerate the economy. I also see as a no-brainer capital <u>investment</u> loans stepped up during a boom and consumption loans <u>drastically reduced</u>. Although this policy by the banking community seems all to obvious, the fact that most people get <u>more</u> and <u>more</u> and <u>more</u> credit card applications during a boom in the economy shows the banking community led by the Federal Reserve Board seems to have the right policy backwards.

Is free trade and NAFTA hurting the US economy? I have heard many people say that NAFTA is hurting American jobs. Free trade and NAFTA are sending jobs overseas to foreign countries. How can Americans complete with low paying foreign workers. This is simply not true. NAFTA and free trade is a great policy it is a great concept for the whole world to benefit. Free trade benefits everyone world trade is good if money sent out to buy foreign goods comes back to buy our American goods. The problem is US interest rates are not free to make this happen. They are regulated by the Federal Reserve and are sometimes used for political purposes. The administration of the 90s jawboned for a strong dollar policy, which the Fed accommodated. This strong dollar policy and tight money gave the US cheap imported goods at a price of severe job loss. In short if the US dollar was where it should be in the foreign exchange markets we as American workers would be the one benefiting from world trade instead of being hurt by it.

A good example of this is in 2003–2004. The dollar has been having a much-needed fall. Only a relatively small drop in the dollar has produced a much greater result. Going into, say, Wal-Mart prior to the 2003–2004 dollar fall, foreign goods were cheap in price but good in quality. After the dollar falling I find the same goods cheap in price but the quality is cheap also. The point is the foreign manufactures and exporters when faced with a falling dollar will have to raise the price and make less profit or lower the quality and make the same profit. If another relatively small fall in the dollar occurs as has happened in 2003-2004 it will make US goods competitive and Wal-Mart may once again have American goods and jobs will be created in the US instead of foreign countries. The dollar needs to decline further <u>slowly</u> and <u>orderly</u>.

Will the Federal Reserve give up the power to regulate interest rates? This is the big question. Even though the Fed has many duties and responsibilities clearing checks, printing money, supplying funds to member banks, jawboning, etc., etc., regulating interest rates is by far their most prestigious function. The function that has the most authority, the most power, the most influence, and the one that keeps them constantly in the limelight. Giving up this function even if the Federal Reserve believed it was in the best interest of the nation would be a hard pill to swallow. But giving up this function they must. In this day and age of free markets and free international trade it is becoming a necessity for them to do so. With the growing global trade of the past years there is no way to avoid severe economic problems and crisis without a free market interest rate policy. Supply and demand for money should regulate interest rates not one person at the Federal Reserve.

Congress created the Federal Reserve and gave it all its powers. Congress must now take away one of its powers, the power to regulate interest rates. Supply and demand should regulate interest rates not the Federal Reserve Board.

So we come to the end of this chapter. Solutions, what can be done?

1.　　The main and most important solution is the Federal Reserve Board must give up the power to regulate interest. Supply and demand for money should regulate interest rates.

2.　　When the Fed has the itchy trigger finger near the top of the business cycle to drop the economy into a recession it should jawbone or use whatever means to convince member bank and other banks, and lending institutions to slowly curtail consumer loans and replace with investment loans. High inflationary consumer spending at the top of a business cycle to be shifted to investment loans that produce more goods and services which lowers inflationary pressures. This policy would be better than a recession.

3. At the same time, as above, when the Fed has the itchy trigger finger they should jawbone the Keynesian Calvary to come to the rescue. All the Keynesian Economists as we know should be advocating a sharply reduced government-spending budget. Since 1936 the Keynesian Economists have advocated high government spending in recessions and low government spending during a boom to prevent inflation. As we know, the Keynesians do tend to forget that second part of the equation. The Federal Reserve could remind them of their philosophy.

4. Allow the dollar to decline slowly and orderly.

5.   Realize that the service industry may make the US wealthy but will not keep the US strong. Massive job losses in autos, high tech, etc., etc., will not keep our status as a strong country.

6.   Realize a dollar to strong or to weak is not good for the American economy. The 70s' weak dollar was just as harmful as the strong 90s' dollar. Free market interest rates will solve that problem.

7.   Realize capital investment is not a bad word. Every time the US economy reaches a capital investment cycle we should not be put into a recession. Let and encourage the economy to shift resources from <u>consumption</u> to <u>capital investment</u>.

8.   Government sectors need to work together on economic issues not against each other. In the business world all departments, accounting, finance, marketing, production, etc., work together for a common strategic plan. When looking at the Federal Reserve and other government sectors they seem at times to be beating up each other instead of working together.

9.   Jawboning, advertising, marketing, these are nice ideas. This could be a new tool of Federal

Reserve policy. If government thinks pollution control is a good idea the first step is legislation and the second step is advertising, marketing, and jawboning to convince the American public. This policy seams to work very well. This could be a new tool for the Federal Reserve to replace the one they should loose.

10.   An additional person to attend all Federal Reserve Board meetings, a person with a knowledge of economics and a genuine concern for the American workers, American investors, American businesses, and all the American people as opposed to just the banking community. Short run banking policies are wrecking the long run banking system. I would volunteer for that position.

A recession, which is the Federal Reserve Board's answer to every economic conundrum (puzzle), is unacceptable.

CHAPTER VIII

GOLD – Investment, Insurance, or Both

Let us start with gold as an investment. Gold is a commodity. It has value for both industrial and financial purposes. It has demand when used in jewelry, plating, and other industrial processes. It has demand also for financial purposes. Coins, bars, and other forms were used around the world throughout history. Throughout the ages, financial crises, political instabilities, wars, and governments creating excess supplies of money have always driven people to invest in gold as a safe haven to protect their wealth. Gold has a relatively fixed supply. Money can be created and printed ad-nauseaum. Because of this reason, people have always turned to this yellow metal for safety during economic uncertainty of inflations and deflations and political uncertainties of wars, revolutions, and civil disorder.

Let us examine economic uncertainties, inflation, deflation, depressions, etc. First, I will start with inflation and deflation, which when out of control both can lead to a depression. In this example there is a fixed money supply, which equals a fixed amount of goods and services and a fixed population. Suppose the Federal Reserve increases the money supply to rapidly, prices will go up in our equation. If the Federal Reserve decreases the money supply to rapidly prices will go down. This is of course, all to obvious. But let us take our same equation and increase goods and services through capital investment prices will fall. People in the economy have more wealth because there are more goods and services with a fixed population. Growing wealth is a growth in goods and services (capital investment) to a fixed population not a growth of money to a fixed population and fixed goods and services.

Another conundrum. During the 1972 presidential election Senator McGovern's platform consisted of a program of a minimum $10,000 a year salary to every American worker, the equivalent to approximately $40,000 today. If you earned $10,000 a year or above you got nothing. If you earned $8,000 a year you received $2,000 from the government. If you did not work you received $10,000 from the government. As a young worker at the time making $7,500 a year the choice was to continue working and receive $2,500 or quit and receive $10,000 salary from the government. Senator

McGovern and his advisors mistakenly thought that growing wealth is a growth of money supply not a growth of goods and services. And after many years of following the Federal Reserve Board's antics, I sometimes believe they don't seam to be aware of this either.

Likewise with a decrease of goods and services, our fixed money supply, and fixed population in our equation, prices rise and our economy becomes poorer. Each time the Federal Reserve Board puts the American economy into a recession, this is precisely what happens. We decrease the amount of goods and services in the economy, and given the fixed money supply and fixed population, the Federal Reserve Board is destroying wealth and setting the stage for much more potential inflation due to less productive capacity in the economy it has created.

Both inflation (rising money supply to a fixed amount of goods and services) and deflation (decreasing money supply to a fixed amount of goods and services) when out of control can lead to a severe depression. We can just define depressions as not a nice time, not a party, not a place to be and leave it like that. No further definition is necessary.

Let us examine political uncertainties; civil disorder, revolution, wars, etc. Throughout history man has had to contend with these problems. In fact, at any given time, these tragedies are occurring somewhere around the globe. I have heard many times by many people, this could not happen in America. This is simply not true. We have, as Americans, been very lucky since WWII that is true. The fact that we as Americans have been strong and wealthy has no doubt helped our luck also. But luck can change, economic instability, can and does create political instability and economic instability is something we are surely facing today if current trends continue. With this said gold is definitely an investment. Gold should have its place in a balanced investment portfolio.

Let us now look at gold as insurance. In our everyday lives almost all of us have insurance. Insurance is a necessity. We have auto insurance, medical insurance, life insurance, business insurance, renter insurance, homeowners insurance, liability insurance, malpractice insurance, disability insurance, etc., etc. Every personal financial planning course and financial planner recognizes the certain need to have insurance to protect your savings and accumulated assets. This fact can hardly be argued.

With the Federal budget deficits as far as the eye can see, Social Security liability looming, massive trade deficits, balances of payments deficits, and massive amounts of dollars held by foreigners (foreign investors and foreign banks) it is very hard for me not to see a need to hold gold as wealth insurance. With this said, gold is definitely insurance. Gold should have its place in a balanced insurance portfolio.

I believe gold is wealth insurance. Anyone who has wealth in the form of bank savings, treasury bills, notes and bonds, corporate bonds, stocks, mutual funds, money market funds, or any other financial instruments and do not own at least 5% gold holdings is driving an auto without auto insurance, living in a home without homeowners insurance, living without life insurance to support your young family and practicing medicine without malpractice insurance. If anyone is not convinced by this book to own gold as an investment it should be clear that gold should be owned as insurance. With this said, I myself believe gold is definitely both an investment and insurance.

Some people refer to someone who advises investing in gold as gold bugs. To me a gold bug is someone who has advised gold purchases over the long term even when its prices has fallen as during the 80s and 90s. Most stock market advisors are stock bugs. They too recommend stock purchases all the time, even when stocks collapse in recessions and the depression. My point here is most financial advisors have a straight line approach to investing. They advise you to buy when something is going up and advise you to buy when it is going down. They always advise you to buy. A better financial advisor would tell you to buy when a financial asset is going up and tell you to sell at the top of the market when the asset is going down.

To show that I am not a gold bug, I purchased gold in 1976 at $120 an ounce. In 1979-1980, gold reached a price of $850 an ounce. I saw the Reagan Administration elected and the Federal Reserve Board policy in 1980 on a mission of tight money and high interest rates. Thinking that policy would stem the weak dollar. I sold gold at $750 an ounce. For twenty years I have not invested in gold or actually recommended gold purchases. But as the dollar has gotten stronger and stronger (much too strong I might add) during the 1990's I have started to believe its time is again coming. Just a few years ago gold drifted to a 20 or so year low of $250 an ounce. I again purchased gold at $277 an ounce. In the last few years gold has been increasing in value to its March 2005 price of $420 an ounce. I believe given the world financial condition and the American financial condition in particular, the price of gold has nowhere to go but upward.

The dollar has strengthened to a level that I believe and government officials have said is unsustainable. This is surely the case. It has strengthened on a very weak foundation as I pointed out earlier. Since this is truly the case, the dollar can only drift down slowly and orderly or collapse. Gold is priced in dollars. If the dollar drifts down slowly and orderly, gold will rise slowly and orderly. If the dollar collapses gold will skyrocket upward. Either case investing in gold or buying gold for wealth insurance is a good investment idea and an investment necessity.

Another point I would like to make about gold is that money equals goods and services. The American economy has money (cash, savings accounts, checking accounts, stocks, bonds, etc.) All these and other financial instruments are claims against all goods and services in the economy. They must equal. The American economy has goods and services (homes, businesses, autos, etc.) Money equals goods and services.

An example of this would be 100 people on Gilligan's Island. If all 100 people only had $1,000 total between them, prices of canoes, huts, fish, etc. would be relatively cheap. A canoe may cost $10; a hut may cost $100. But suppose Chatsworth Osborne, Jr., brought with him $1,000,000 in cash to divide up for the 100 people on the island. Prices would be different. Huts would be $100,000; perhaps, a canoe may cost $2,000, etc., etc. Money equals goods and services.

Let us take this example one step further. If money equals goods and services and the dollar collapses or people loose confidence in it as in Germany after WWI then gold would equal goods and services. Since there is approximately $25,000 in money (currency, savings, checking accounts, money market accounts, etc.) to every ounce of gold (at the Federal Reserve Bank, Fort Knox, private investors, mining companies, investment companies, etc., etc.) it is plain to see that gold would rise to the incredible price of $25,000 an ounce if the dollar became worthless and gold was to be substituted for it.

I do not foresee this happening as such with certainty but I do see a real very real possibility of a dollar collapse and this disaster coming to fruition. I do see the dollar falling from its height that is unsustainable and pushing gold to levels that make today's price look very, very cheap. Given the possibility of a dollar collapse it would be foolish not to own gold as an investment, insurance, and both.

A footnote to this chapter regarding money equals goods and services. I disagree with economists on what qualifies as money. I list as money, M1, M2, M3, but I also listed bonds, stocks, notes, and other financial instruments. My reasoning is, if I have $1,000 in my pocket as cash I have money. If I put the $1,000 in the bank checking account I still have money. If I buy a $1,000 US Savings Bond, I still have money. If I buy a corporate stock, I still have money. If I buy a money market mutual fund I still have money. All these financial instruments are owned by people who think they have money. If the dollar looses its credibility, safety, value, usefulness, etc. These people will sell these instruments to get their money back. The next step will be to purchase gold as real money.

If I am going to invest 5% of my portfolio in gold what is the best vehicle I should use? Should I buy a gold mutual fund? Should I buy gold coins? Bars? Gold stocks? Gold options? Gold futures? etc. etc. While there are some exceptions the recommended 5% of portfolio value for investment and insurance purposes should be in gold bullion coins, taken delivery and stored in a safe deposit box at a bank. The three best gold bullion coins are, in my opinion, the one once Canadian Maple Leaf, the one ounce American Eagle, and the one ounce Austrian Philharmonic. These coins can be purchased through Monex (www.monex.com

or calling Greg Morton at 1-800-949-4653, ext. 2285) or other reputable gold dealer or coin shop. Monex Deposit Company has been in business since 1967 and I use them for my purchases. You can also open an IRA and purchase these gold coins at Monex, which must be stored, in their vaults if an IRA account. Another exception is very wealthy individuals would have 400 ounce bars stored in vaults.

Another exception would be if you really felt very certain of gold increasing in value as I do, you could purchase more than the recommended 5% or use additional funds for investment in gold mutual fund or gold mining stocks. One very, very important reason I like the gold bullion coins mentioned above is they have a face value and they are legal tender coins. The Canadian Maple Leaf and the American eagle have a $50 face value and the Austrian Philharmonic has a 100 Euros face value, which is about $130 American. This means it cannot go below 100 Euros. This makes theses gold bullion coins a great investment and I will explain why.

A great technique in investing is averaging down. You buy a stock at $20 a share it goes up you make money. The stock falls to $10 a share you buy more. The stock falls to $5 a share you buy much more. The stock falls to $1 a share, you buy much, much, much, more. When the stock finally goes up you have made a whole lot of money. Great, Huh!! Right!!!

As we know this technique can blow up in your face when the stock is worthless. The company files bankruptcy, etc. This cannot happen with gold bullion coins. You can purchase your coins and keep averaging your little touché all the way down to the minimum face value legal tender amount struck on the face of the coin. And if gold ever reached that low figure, the economy would be so prosperous the rest of your portfolio would be successful, more than making up for any fall in gold prices. You would be smoking the very best Cuban cigars.

What is the chance of political instability in the United States of America? Political instability (as defined as civil disorder, anarchy, riots, revolution, chaos, etc.) by itself and in itself seems pretty slim. We in America have a relatively stable political system when compared to other nations. But if we in American have economic instability (defined as severe inflation, deflation, depression, dollar collapse, etc.) we raise the chance of political instability to near 90% and the chance of economic instability today is very, very much greater than most people realize or comprehend. The fact then that economic instability is high if current trends continue, and economic instability surely leads to political instability.

We now arrive at my thesis that the threat of economic and political instability is growing in this country if current trends continue. I want to reiterate the point that it is not inevitable only based on current trends continuing. As pointed out earlier, sometimes in history trends change and sometimes they don't.

I would like to make one more point on this particular issue. Who would have thought Russia would have imploded? I didn't think so! The only person I knew that thought that was my father in the early seventies. Russia and the US were the world's superpowers and the two greatest economic nations at that time. I would be willing to bet not many Russians felt that it could possibly happen either. But it did and it could happen in the US also.

How did it happen in Russia? The chance of political instability in Russia was very slim. The communist government had a good control of the political system. But economic instability leads to political instability and Russia was vulnerable to economic instability just as we are today. The Reagan Administration pumped up the economy in the

80s. With a strong economy his administration pumped up the military also. With a strong economy that can easily be done. The Russians trying to match the US military spending without a strong economy to generate that spending, Russia implodes.

The Reagan administration in my opinion achieved many goals and was the best administration in all of the 20th century. Imploding Russia, although not very good for the Russian people, leaving the United States as the only standing superpower was surely a good goal from our perspective. Stopping the trend towards runaway inflation in 1980 that could have turned easily to civil disorder was another achievement to Reagan's credit. Anyone following politics and economics in the late 70s knew that was a distinct possibility.

Why do people make economic or political predictions that do not always come true? The answer is most predictions, both economic and political, are based on current trends continuing in the same manner into the future. The problem is sometimes trends change direction, political leaders also see the problems arise and make the necessary changes to avoid the problem. Sometimes the people force the change in a predicted trend and sometimes the predictions come true.

In 1977, I predicted runaway inflation (economic instability) creating civil disorder (political instability), in this country. I had purchased gold in 1976 at $120 an ounce and knew if current trends continued there was no doubt in my mind that this dire prediction would come to fruition. With current trends continuing and a second term of President Carter I was investing all my savings in gold. I also advocated at that time to purchase a second home in the mountains as a retreat, which was rare then but common today. This practice today has many reasons, one of which is the economic and political instability people see coming today.

So what happened to the prediction that I made in 1977? Was I wrong? Not really!! 1977 through 1980 saw economic conditions worsening. Inflation was climbing rapidly. The dollar was falling rapidly, political and economic instability was mounting and gold was climbing to $850 an ounce. When I saw Ronald Reagan elected president with his economic advisors like Professor Milton Freidman and others, I knew the trend was going to change. Shortly after the election when I saw the trends were changing in a different direction, I sold my gold holdings at $750 an ounce. I told everyone that knew of my 1977 prediction that my

Moosehead Lake Cottage was now going to be for recreation not retreat.

Some trends do change and some trends don't change. If the Federal Reserve Board does not heed the information advice and warnings in this book, please <u>reread</u> this chapter "Gold – Investment, Insurance or Both."

A recession, which is the Federal Reserve Board's answer to every economic conundrum (puzzle), is unacceptable.

POSTSCRIPTS

- I am very glad the Social Security money was not invested in the stock market as President Clinton purposed during his administration in the 90s.

- If the United States ever had to go to war with one of its major trading partners, they would not have to fight us. The country could sell dollars on the foreign exchange markets, collapsing our financial system, and win without firing a shot if current trends continue.

- I believe economics should be taught in every grade of grammar school and high school. It also should be required for every major in college. I have been adamant about this since the early 70s. I witnessed a significant increase of economics pushed forth during the later stages of the Reagan administration, but it is still miniscule compared to what it should be. Please cut back on the art, music, gym, etc., etc., and increase the most important subject economics. More wars have been started over ignorance in economics second only to religion.

- I was watching a program on National Geographic where some scientists entered a cave to study bats. As they were walking in the cave all the bats were hanging upside down perfectly still. There were millions of bats. All of a sudden a few started to move then fly. Then a few more, then incredible amounts of bats, millions, flew out of the cave. At that point all I could think of was the incredible amount of dollars hanging upside down in the foreign exchange markets, like bats in a cave.

- Even though supply side theory was labeled trickle down economics, the real trickle down economics is Keynesian Theory. Keynesian Theory hands out fish while supply side theory teaches you to fish.

- Keynesian Theory, though needed during the Great Depression should have been disposed of properly in 1939.

- The Federal Reserve does not fight inflation the Federal Reserve causes inflation. Inflation says "you pay me now or you pay me later." With the 1960s and 1970s Federal Reserve policy, inflation had a pay me now effect. Inflation showed immediately. With the 1990s and 2000s Federal Reserve policy inflation has a pay me later effect.

Current trends continuing the dollar collapse will be the pay me later effect of this 15 year monetary explosion.

- We know "Says" Law states supply creates it's own demand, but "Johnny's" Law states that if supply and demand for a resource are not left alone to function short run policy goals will create the exact <u>opposite</u> long run policy effects. This includes interest rates.

- A house in my old neighborhood just sold. It was built in the 1930's for $2,000, sold in the 1950's for $10,000, and today for $250,000. Why did the same house rise in price from $2,000 to $250,000? Let's assume the population triples during that time period and the quantity of goods and services triples and the money supply triples also. That house today would still sell for $2,000. These three factors are in balance. But if one of the three variables increases or decreases at a higher percentage relative to the others, prices will rise or fall accordingly. The percentage growth of the money supply by the Fed during that period <u>by far</u> surpassed the percentage growth of population and the percentage growth of the quantity of goods and services. That's why that house today sold for $250,000.

- The Rolling Stones, the greatest musical group that ever existed, the real kings of Rock and Roll. It was a real good idea to knight Mick Jagger. It was a real bad idea to knight Alan Greenspan.

- I would like to compare the 60's and 70's Federal Reserve Board to the 90's and 2000's Federal Reserve Board. In the 70's the Fed had an easy money policy, pumping money into the system at an incredible rate. As the money filtered into the economy prices started to rise. Interest rates would then start to rise also after prices. The Fed would then keep interest rates below what the market interest rates would have been. "Behind the Curve" was the term used to describe this situation. Inflation showed immediately. The 90's Fed also pumped money into the system at an incredible rate. Just like the 70's, as the money filtered into the economy prices would start to rise. Then interest rates would start to rise also. At this point the 90's Fed would raise interest rates faster than what the market interest rates would have been. "Ahead of the Curve" is the term and difference between the two policies. This policy with above market interest rates produced a strong dollar, which sent dollars out of the country rather than translating to domestic inflation.

Inflation is postponed like "millions of bats hanging in a cave." If supply and demand regulated interest rates, rates would be always "on the curve." Not behind, not ahead, but right on.

- Did the Federal Reserve Board cause World War II? The Fed interest rate and monetary policy mistakes of the 1920's caused the Great Depression of the 1930's. The depression caused World War II. Events influence other events. Economic instability dramatically increases the chance of political instability. One of the purposes of this book is to prevent that from happening again or at least, push the potential event further and further into the future instead of pulling it into the present. Let's learn from the past.

- "Money Supply Matters" and " Free Market Interest Rates Matter." Two very important sides of the monetary responsibility coin.

- Warning this book contained economic information, economic advice, economic history, economic humor, economic rhetoric, and economic entertainment. All designed for the sole purpose to get people to want to read this book and make the necessary changes that must be done for the benefit of all. Economics when understood is not the dismal science.

About the Author

John Shannon attended colleges in Boston, Massachusetts during the 1960's majoring in Accounting. His first taste of investing came in 1973 during the stock market crash of that time. He opened his first account at Merrill Lynch in Burlington, Massachusetts putting all his savings in stocks selling at $1 a share.

Watching the stocks rising in value, and not knowing when or if he should sell, he dusted off his old college Economics textbook and read from cover to cover with a greater interest than ever before. After numerous trips to the Harvard Book Store to purchase many used Economics books, John spent an average of 6 hours a day in the local public libraries during a 5-year period from 1973 to 1978, reading textbooks, as well as, the Wall Street Journal, Business Week, and other periodicals.

Economics and investing became a passion. In 1976 selling stocks at the top of the market and buying gold at $120 an oz, which turned out to be the near low for gold, was the next financial step. In 1980, when the Regan administration was elected he decided that the gold price would fall so he sold his gold holdings at $750 an oz.

John successfully predicted the real estate market collapse in 1988 and the stock market crash of 2000. He has been recommending buying gold recently since it's low price of $277 an oz a few years ago. In the mid 1980's, he was a registered investment advisor for a short period of time.

www.ingramcontent.com/pod-product-compliance
Lightning Source LLC
Chambersburg PA
CBHW022020170526
45157CB00003B/1302